Glass Cassowary

Biographies

Robert Verdon

Robert Verdon's published works include *A Spiral Life* (Resurgam Press), *My Cat Eats Spaghetti* (Ginninderra Press), and *Her Brilliant Career* (Aberrant Genotype Press). His poetry can be found in *Overland*, *The Blue Nib*, *Cordite*, etc. He worked as Literary Editor of *Muse* and with Aberrant Genotype Press. He has a PhD in English (University of Canberra).

Kate McNamara

Kate McNamara is a playwright, poet and critical theorist. Her works include *Leaves, The Rule of Zip* and *The Void Zone* (Aberrant Genotype). Her editorial credits include *When Angels Call* (Craig Cormick, Aberrant Genotype) and *The Lace Maker* (Kathy Kituai, Ginninderra). She co-edited *Black Lives, Rainbow Visions* (Jenni Kemarre Martiniello, Black Ink).

Glass Cassowary

Robert Verdon

Edited by Kate McNamara

GLASS CASSOWARY

Poems by Robert Verdon

Edited by Kate McNamara

ISBN 9781763825949

Walleah Press
South Launceston
Tasmania, Australia 7249
www.walleahpress.com.au
ralph.wessman@walleahpress.com.au

Table of Contents

Fishing, with my father

The canoe was almost underwater
We paddled to a sandy sliver
Dad and me with rods for slaughter
Of flathead in the Mogo River.
No stars above us but the one,
The clouded early-morning sun.
And on the sandbank we caught more
— The stupid rivalry in me
Forgotten, this close to the sea —
Fish than we ever had before.

Goulburn Crow

On a wire
at the edge of historic Goulburn
a crow clad in air the hue of a clean dishcloth
bright fog moving in
sings for me
unknowingly
with a silent chorus of smaller birds.
I answer with a cough or two;
more birds
wheel and mutely gather as
the lathered morning leaps into day.
The crow's short croak is
almost like the sounds
made by water dripping through a live light socket,
far more mysterious and numinous —
then I look up up up
the crow is gone

Currawong

Currawong clearing
up the cat food
How can I be old
When I watch you like a child?

glass cassowary
for Paul Klee & Walter Benjamin

The dreamt past
subtly chokes me:
a glass cassowary, with diamond-fire
on each spined wingtip,
the new Angel of History,

Slides into the slippery present …
a memory-play in amber, a closet drama,
a cacophony of monologues.
Seals of grey cloud whales across the
end of the pinched avenue.

It is coastal weather now, east wind in treetown,
and I am back to saving five-dollar notes;
I drop one down the back of the horizon and,
surprising as the discovery that cobweb
feels like fairy-floss,

Or that objects I pick up talk back and
complain they are now conscious
and need to be left alone,
it spins like a sycamore seed
or a galaxy.

The wind comes impossibly from every place
of suffering, each curbside Golgotha,
each insect trodden on, each baby
abandoned under rubble. I am an insect
with prescience, shut out from each side, blown away.

The wasted future is all dream:
heroic leaders and cracked-mirror rivals invest in dragon's teeth,
savaging the soiled soles of street-dwellers, while
robot shop assistants in synthetic heels telegraph dark factories,
and my mind occasionally lassos

a glass cassowary
(a vicious bird)
by a smattering
of threatened rainforest trees
so tall they take

holy water
straight out of
the pelmetted
pregnant
clouds

I hang out the washing on it
surprised, again,
by the velvet apocalypse growl
and perspex-glint
of a light plane

at 11 o'clock
as a badly disciplined
white formation
of drunken ducks splattered with bloody sunset,
chased by the shattering cassowary,

crosses out the high
blue fields
heading north in Summer.

orphan

mynah swoops young pee-wee
as I feed its hunting, haunted mother
bits of bread and peanut butter

as I squawk
all three fly off
two across the pool

later
I backstroke
under a feathery blue sky

hanging from a spider thread

like a fallen leaf
spinning in a secret breeze

tracing
an imaginary line
from my navel to a hidden star

Elegy for a Cat [1]

To Cobber

Before the garden grave
by the path you knew
and the house wall
in your territory
of the world and universe, you,
black fur soaked,
had died in your sleep
facing east, crag-still:
a hot night that turned
to cold funeral rain,
like midnight birdsong,
escaping the boundary,
escaping mortality,
escaping lameness and pain.
Here lies Cobber —
What can be said
For the timeless, numberless,
unspecified dead.

---

[1] 'Here lies … cat' — Kenneth Mackenzie, 'Derelict',
Selected Poems of Kenneth Mackenzie,
ed. Douglas Stewart,
Sydney: Angus and Robertson, 1961, p152

Last Wednesday

To Eileen O. Verdon, 27th January 1919 — 15th June 2021

O my mother
all night
so small on
that cold floor

the last fall,
into the abyss
or the arthritic hand of
God

O my mother
you who hated doctors

      once, you
         fell out of the high bed
      and broke your front milk teeth
         raced down the Voylart hill
      on a scooter, spooking a pony and trap
         stood barely five foot high surrounded by yellow gunpowder
      and detonators in the Arsenal, snug in the hidden valley, beneath
      Heinkel or Junkers drone, towered over and hating the shoes you
      had to share, warm from another's feet
      before Australia

now
still as the
walking frame
behind you

O my mother

found,
by me,
a lost child

Sixty-Two

       Another bloody birthday
hardly seems worth the
celebration of it

another step closer
      o fabulosa
to the end

waking before dawn
once again I must choose
      between candles or cake —

as absurd and unpoetic as the
abolition of death
by Technology.

Rising Early on My 70th

The pre-dawn has flown faster than I know:
Here's me, letting the cat out, flicking the
Light-switch up and down, bedazzled by confusion,
Trying to turn off the sun.

never abolish chance

sometimes
things bounce off me
no matter what
they are —
a woman
bright and
80 or so
pushing a
mean walker
spoke to me
outside the
Post Office
in Dickson
as I looked at
books reduced
'I remember
after the war
— the Second
World War'
she added
as if it could
be the First,
or maybe
Vietnam, I
suppose
'my father
taught me to
use a
typewriter …'
so she came to
school with
typewritten
sheets, despite
a broken arm,
scandalising
the teacher,

'and there weren't
many books
around then — oh, there
were a few …
he taught me
how to do cryptic
crosswords when
I was seven …'
Kate would be
waiting
this lady probably
had to go too
her speech was
coherent, but
not my memory of it,
the queue in
the post office
was long
and stifling
but it was
nice to be
welcomed
into the company
of my fellow
geriatrics
even if
they are still
older than me,
even in the cemetery
I will be
'the baby of the group'.
For no reason
I recall now
that the 'natives'
in a certain jungle
smash their enemies'
heads with clubs so heavy
that nothing remains but shrapnel.
I wish her long life,
whatever happens
to mine.

Moment of passing by

Old figure
White head bent so low
That from behind,
You seem headless,
Making sure the stick's ferrule
Evades the drain cover,
Under a grille of branches:
Sparrow in a cold wind,
In March, third decade in.

the spoon twists

as one of my Welsh ancestors said,
his English poor,
to the woman at the Ritz

—— he had won a meal there
for himself and the family ——

as she cast about for something
to stir her coffee with,
while he proffered the very item

excuse me, Madam
you may 'ave my spoon
I 'ave twisted my tea.

Baseball Caps

nearly died once
who hasn't, they shrug,
you'll get it right next time
life goes on
so do cars and bicycles and wind-bells and clichés
in my street
on and on
like a droning preacher or P.M.
a siren whistles and waffles
death beckons
I feel like rowing a boat down the main drag
like de Nerval taking his lobster for a walk
there is potential outside my window
yet no one knows it
and it seems the whole bloody world wears baseball caps.

The Wayward Girl

the umbra of her life
the years of scorn and ridicule,
when she brought into disrepute
'the moral tone of the skewl',

was no justification of her improprieties
would not be considered by the Board
could never be illuminated
let justice be done and the girl ignored

the shadow on the impassive face
of Mr Justice _____ ten years hence
was her own, but of course at law
a shadow
is no defence

Not All Men

not all men built patriarchy

let alone ran it
not my father nor my uncles
nor my grandfather who died at 41 in any case
      my mother's father who
        in solidarity with his fellow Welsh coal-miners
        rather than call the strike-breaking police
        beat the shit out of the man who beat his wife
        who then took it out on his wife

Justice

You killed my son!

he echoed for twenty years,
vile as Henry VIII in that old show,
till with his fingerprints all over me
I stabbed him with the dressmaking shears
in what was left of his heart.

here the dance is
the barred sun tumbling into senescence
the trees full of children

Twenty eternities later
I sleep a whole night now
in the farthest corner of my cell.

garden days (2021)

Have I cut my finger
As I break off sorrel leaves?
No, it is just the red juice,
The consistency and colour of blood.
Earlier, uprooting superfluous seedlings,
I apologise under my breath for healthy murder.
Witlessly anthropomorphic,
I will never make a gardener.
But what else, three years off
Seventy, but to cultivate
your own grave?

garden days (2024)

the road to the stars
is a human hair curving off the world

into another atmosphere
rendering rockets obsolete

but it is hard to find this road
and as hard to fathom and spooky

as quantum entanglement
or love between children

when you do
you spring up into an equivalent garden

in a tracery of new history
under a red sun

cradling a blue flower
among friends powerful as gods.

Another Missed Opportunity

Inside a cold space at the top of a water tower
the alien hides, protected by a force-field
powered by whatever's thrown at it, but
still is terrified to go out in case it gives itself
away … it can only eat rhubarb on this planet
and looks like a rat, though as large as a camel,
and cannot change shape as in the movies,
and though it speaks 100 earth languages like a native
and has the secret of eternal life, the philosopher's stone
and a few other goodies ten-a-penny at home
and worth oilfields here, it has frozen … maybe nobody
deserves these gifts (as its predecessors claimed) and in any
case it has a classic case of new-planet agoraphobia …
the ship *can* change shape and after a few days the water
tower blasts off again, headed for the centre of the galaxy.

Utopian piano

whenever I think of pianos
I think of fieldmice
sleeping in the folds of the prairie
and gyroscopes
ladling vanilla brooks
into rockpools, by a wolf
extending a paw to the universe:
but that's just me

Bumper Stickler

in the bowling alley
noisy with youth
we, white
-haired, were
asked if we wanted 'bumpers'
by a tall smiling youth,
low railings such as they give
to small children
to stop the bowl spinning off
the lane

we declined and
sent the moment
into the gutter

yokels

bars
long afternoon shadows
where the southern desert begins
sheep's skulls reflections and
sunlight sheers off what
seem puddles of coffee
we were told he killed his victims
('only thirty years ago')
with a purple sweet potato and then
ate the murder weapon
now we wait for the light plane
out of here
where the sky is as tall as the tales
and the folks stand eye to eye with the aurora

the continuity of personality

no respect for public housing
said my father
they piled building waste on
top of our lavender bush
just one of those trivial things
that stick in the memory

Class

class is the pointed golden arch
        from which
                all bigotry hangs
                        its enemies —
                no wonder
        they
don't mention it

Fine and Private Places

walking up the peeling bare flagpole
of the shut-down state school
the fly sees many schools

through its compound eyes
the ones that might have been
and might still be, the schools

(or hospitals, or scientific
institutions) that might improve
our short lives on this earth,

or even lengthen them;
of course, the fly fails to grasp
the significance of all this,

as far as we know, and is soon a-buzz
within the house of a local worthy
whose maid swiftly sprays it stone dead.

We Pledge to Thee[1]

… with a forties God above,
Brylcreemed in an Air Marshall's uniform
to ladle out the weather,
I walk through the bunyip cloisters
of Telopea Park High School
(where some of the boys wear dresses),
hair cascading down my back to defy the Principal,
not dreaming I'd be living in the
same dreary megavillage fifty years later,
beneath the Brylcreemed God of fifty years earlier.

---

[1] Title from the old Telopea Park High School Song,
sung to the tune of 'The Red Flag' / 'O Tannenbaum'.

Rubber Hand[2]

the rubber hand illusion
of modern politics
makes *parliament* into
something representative
as you watch it vote
but we know what's what
till it's hit with a hammer.

---

[2] cf https://www.youtube.com/watch?v=sxwn1w7MJvk [6.7.2024]

Bell

bell, bell

stiff as an old heart
clamorous as a tin clock
raw as a resonant pun

every prayer is not useless
echoes the Great Bell of Moscow,

the cracked Liberty Bell,
the Maria Dolens,

and tocsins, sleigh bells, crotal bells, the bells of Hell,
anthems for doomed youth,

even *Bella Ciao Ciao Ciao!* —
bell, bell, bell, bell, bell

toll for me.

destroying angel

heavy-fisted rain is falling
on the tin roof, on the street
colder as the heart is crawling,
voices wailing, trampling feet
hear the drumming of its fingers
hear the silences between
feel the echoing that lingers
rain a razor, wet and keen
over, over, beating metal
roof sings like a copper bowl
sound as perfect as a petal
penetrating to the soul
several grey bedraggled figures
children by the Gazan wall
in the lifeless arms of parents:
Son of Shoah's come to call.

Panzers on Fire

jangling propaganda they shriek
several days a week
blond child against Asiatic steel

lying in a rusty pool
drowning in
the decrepitude of empires

faint echoes of the metal roar
across the borderland
of milk and honey

the Panzer men of old
singing lustily for Bandera
ripping out throats as they go

Slava Ukraini! fighting the last war
and vapourising
in the next one

The Stockman Train, 2017

went on an old train today
from Canberra's dinky railway station
should have been steam but a last-minute substitution
rendered it 'heritage diesel', an old shunting engine by the look of it

you could actually open the window
an old sash-type window
and the carriages squeaked less than the ageing XPT
quite a few oldies aboard
oldies running it too
like being aboard a big old caravan
though the wooden fittings had been
replaced by plastic fakery in the seventies

we learned *inter alia*
that Fyshwick
the industrial suburb we passed through
had been a P.O.W. camp
for Germans in the First World War
that the folks in the *Headquarters Joint Operations Command* that we also passed
worked literally underground
that the carriages had once served as rail-ambulances
saving wounded soldiers from the added injuries caused by Sydney's wartime roads
some of which were made with half-sunk wooden blocks

went on an old train today
wind blowing through for air-conditioning
shot through three tunnels
more leisurely arrow than bullet
so bicycle-slow on the hills
you could almost pick the wildflowers
and so noisy the cows ran from us
people waved as we passed
the horn was tooted
the kids loved it

went on an old train today
it goes to Bungendore village every third Sunday
somehow the journey delighted
more than the destination

Dickson, Thursday

Suddenly,
protected from the rain,
the old man playing the
psychedelic street piano,
sad as the dead,
in Dickson
where the beggars
drink in doorways
to Christmas,
normal for once,
stretching out
beneath the bountiful hand
of goblin commerce,
and the clenching tears take me,

I am in another city,
in the warping sun,
another story,
another chance
…

Last Night in Dickson

last night in Dickson
a familiar
beggar outside Woolies,
in this rich town —
this time I gave
nothing, he called out
to no one in particular,
do you want to buy a poem?

it's time

when the stooped man with stringy hair
shuffling again from his dressing room,
the Gents
in front of the O'Connor shops,
tentatively sings *a cappella* under a tree,
in perhaps Polish after too much Smirnoff,
an old black beret at his feet

when farther south I know
the dark woman pushes
her top-heavy shopping trolley
across Commonwealth Bridge
between Civic and the House
while in the lower circles of empire
the future perishes at the breast

when secure cranes multiply
devouring the old, baby-faced city
and the unlucky ghosts of what was
hide like escaped mental patients
in my room all day long
as I finger-pick my '68 guitar
and Mt Ainslie 'roos crop the lawn

when the prospect for baby is
a broken glass mother
exhumed from the demolished house
at the alien end of the lane,
a Hanged Man destined for an icy tombstone
or a 24 karat apartment tower
babbling in the hot wind

when the snow is dry
as dandruff
and the leaves paper-dead
while the thimble bells ring
dead as silver or lead
in the bent steeples
of skeleton fingers

when there is vertigo atop
bullet-riddled markets,
jagged razor curves of growth
soft as gold in the green sprouting,
that latticed time of tears
when synaptic arpeggios falter
and graveyards tremble

then an exploring infant
finger
writes a new script
drawing down the moon
in a nascent language,
toppling the glass towers
like dominoes.

Cameo

… along the drying nature strip
looking for miniature moons
in the dying couch grass, hoping
for edible suns, rare coins,
glacé cake ornaments,
emeralds and rubies,
old school photos,
special dispensations,
lucky breaks,
windfalls,
fingerprints of destiny,
faces of the future.

A blind Barmecide utopia.

He wouldn't really wish for the moon
It'd be like living in Broken Hill.

His face is as ragged as his
ashen school jumper with the
green and yellow
stripes
round the collar.

He has the winning Lotto ticket
but doesn't know it.

This is where he lives
and dies

My City

muscle memory maps of
old routes I have taken
in my little, new, adopted city
where people have lived
for thousands of millennia

down the ramp to Adelaide Avenue
onto the freeway built in 1965
round to Curtin by the old school
or back at Kallaroo Road, Pialligo,
bleak and lonely on the farm

while alien and primordial
within a planted forest
coeval with the angels,
at night they comfort
like breathing

Canberra

apart from trees,
there are few

monuments in this
theme park city

this gilded village
this bush retreat

of graphite roads
through paper parks

a drawing board
come almost to life

exciting
as voting

and clean
as plastic

ideal
as the digital

a revolution
safe in bed

socialism and drains
now only drains

awash with freeways
devoid of trains

(controversy mainly
involves the tram)

a plumber's paradise
a developer's dreamscape

a thousand suburbs
caged in ennui

estranged
from the deep earth

and the environs
of stars

monument, so far
to the defeat of idealism

downunder

over the balcony railing
of Hadley's Hotel in Hobart
rebuked by the blond bulk of St David's
the sea breeze comes caressing
the new millennium
and I am scared of heights

I walk about striving
not to step on Australiana
or spear kookaburra dreams,
my thongs spattered with red mud,
my bloody history losing itself
like rain on a terracotta road

tomorrow night we'll
spend
in the casino

Central Coast

Dark in the afternoon
the tunnel went on

an ancient night with no sunrise —
Then, out of the WestConnex,
we joined a peri-urban sprawl,
a surprise, a city I'd never heard of,
where strange signs proclaimed
luminous dentistry plain jane's fashions anglers war
('ehouse' painted faintly a layer beneath) —
we laughed too at the latticework
eye(sore) of Sauron, a great mast
poking up near The Entrance —
but we had come, eclipsed, to visit the sick.

The heart quivers like a faltering hand.

I met a green lizard by the steep bank
in the Wyong Hospital carpark.
Hope comes early with rosy fingers.
There were conifers of bellbirds nearby,
each with its own note tall as a tree,
hanging in unearthly cadences.

The YTI

In Little Bourke St we stay
At the YTI Garden Hotel,
Round the corners, no garden but Italian restaurants,
Their staff with Indian accents,
And of course coffee emporia …
People walk so much, ignoring side-alleys of high-class graffiti
Ubers stop just past the door.

Night passes off like a headache
We sleep on unhindered by direct sun
Due to a light well with cigarette butts,
Immured as houseplants; the man
On reception is always smiling.
Only the shrieks of drunks and sirens
Penetrate the walls.

Melbourne / *Naarm:*
No longer just a good place
To make a film about
The end of the world

When I saw Russia for the First Time

when I saw Russia as if for the first time
in a slide at nightschool
(failing to stick out my Higher School Certificate
in the grim days before I had a degree
and the sea-veneer of worldliness)
it was so green

not red, or the gunmetal, prison-colour
I had expected
despite a smattering of Marx and Lenin

1972

Mother Russia was just a girl
sticking it out on the turned earth
on a country road, far from all innocence

all was future then

down from the country capital
in Sydney, alone
dizzily peering up at tall buildings
fresh off the bus, hope
an opal between its treads
down by Circular Quay
billboards for Dewars Whisky
and Red Mill Rum
ferry to the Zoo, mind
taut as a canvas sail
a rainbow in a magnifying glass
no one at all bothered me
the battens were set
at last, I was free
it might have been Dublin
sailing through
ideas for great architecture
architecture as frozen revolution
tall as the bald towers
and the sky jigsawed by rooftops
into silent oratorios
I might have stood unknowingly
not far from where Henry Lawson
(whose book I had from Uncle Jack)
once stood to cadge pennies for drink
and with some inkling
of being a poet

1967, thirteen,
all was future then,
though not just for me.

neighbourly babel

that neighbourly babel
I hear, the clinking of bottles cascading
into the bin, the drunk father or daughter
pounding the locked door as the other snores within,
the echo of weekday parties writ small,
the hung over silence of early morning,
the old folks hobbling and avoiding a fall,
shuffling along the path with walkers dodging
skateboards, *clickety-clack*
the men (and one woman) with their monotonic roar of
leaf-blowers chainsaws whipper-snippers
airrrrrrrrrrrrrrrrrrrrrrrrrrrrrrrrrrrrrrrrrrrrrrrr —
galling, airless
the noisy mynahs and cockatoos out the back and
quarrelling possums (till someone rang the department)
the traffic in the offing, rising and falling like breath
and hear the here and there of a light plane
or a knock on a door, even my own or
a squeak of speaking snow or sand, but that's in my head —
the language of sound that, unlike light,
only touches us when something is going on (the possums are back)
behind, above, or dead ahead.

Anzac Day figment

As poodles, one black,
one white, look on,
the old folks
sit around a long table in the granny flat,
guzzling Anzac biscuits,
brownies and coffee,
sharing out parts
from *Much Ado About Nothing*,
not apportioning vital resources
like sharp-clad bankers:
meanwhile, the younger generation
is on holiday, and
plans the further enhancement
of the dual occupancy.
As they emerge, three F-18s
rocket overhead.

bright

in a distant corner of the country
soaring white blossoms on a dead tree
spied from the Cootamundra-Harden train
a flock of cockatoos
rising in a stilled-sea landscape
of gentle, folded, fecund hills,
planted in memory forever.

spring

as the chilly wheel buckles …

from the rock, banded by iron drought
from   the dry rot of winter
from   the hard enclosing garden walls

of stunted ranges
each peak a balletic point of morning dream
of distant mandolins of mist, fleeting as a bird in a mirror,
pirouetting on the surface of a fingerling stream
as you open your eyes, throat tinder, and lost

— a mast, the sky sways,
a vein, the sky swells,
the dark park branches
blossom with dawn
over the jagged benches
transitory
with the sigh of a brassy blast —

it comes
the wheel heaves out of a rut

      water is sweet
      once more,
      and the rain is not vinegar
      the sun rolls too quickly
      along the ecliptic

night highway to paradise

night highway to paradise
slalom conversations under the cold wound of stars
we eat a lot as the heater is broken
there's no need for the convertible's roof down
it feels like 1963 but it isn't
we each feel like Kennedy
in the tightest part of each curve
there crouches the dark stranger
whose eye glitters like a tooth
the brakes shriek, on the drums
the starfields are a long roll
from hi-hat to snare to tom-toms
— or vice-versa —
right into the cornice of the winter
a gaping clash of darknesses
as the cat's eyes shoot past …

the green fortress

here, sentinel roses nod
at the gate of the green fortress
the tree in the cemetery
where my parents rot
none shall pass
time is a globe, or a rose root, or
seaweed on a wave leaping taller than me

mother
father
children
cats
transformed into whispers
and passers-by at a distance
on Mayday screens

dreams and miracles are wrought in soil
and river and sea
and like all mighty works
run into the sand
as time grows in every direction

still I believe in the future

Shipping

shrubs flutter, hushed by our window-pane
in the sky
white vessels steam slowly by
never stopping at our port
we lie
imprisoned in our garden city on a hill
pretending it is a futuristic airship or levistat or Laputa
skyline not yet built into battlements
open as a wound or a window
shining
little to do
in the butter-bean morning
but watch the shipping

Risen Shadow

and
the blue
-green
eucalypt,
a white
fountain
of flowers in
early May

death row

we have seen water come out of a rock
and children disappear into it
nothing removes the stain
not even ozone from the blood-brown rattler trains of youth
while progress is a sad nosewheel turning on a remote runway
here, where even plumb-bobs and sundials fail
and water freezes in the earth's veins

nothing removes the stain, the streak, the shriek …

sunless shadows sprout in my windowbox
overlooking a windblown town of squat ungreened towers
sheltering long-shadowed figures with tricycle prams as
sweltering trams clatter past and stained freeways hover in old fog
and in this unthinking city of the eye open seven days
I drift off the edge, bleeding fast
into unruffleable feathers of finger-laid stone, archipelagos of misfit moments

unassuming as a bent row of thin, unlined coffins
nothing, no atom of shadow, ever removes the stain
as we are snuffed out by heaving ingots of sunshower
rearranging the draped furniture hopefully in our cells
dreaming bleeding dreams, that cut-price laundry of the soul —
nothing

yet

removes the stain
the praeternatural shame
of the

honest execution.

light and life

looking through a cracked window,
always in my own light

… a striped iceberg light,
a strange arpeggio

a lightning flash hissing close
in its own light

light and life is too much for me
suicide is meaningless

I wish my critics only immortality

Acknowledgements

These poems have appeared previously, or been entered in competitions.Some have been revised.

orphan | *Shortlisted in 2021 Bruce Dawe National Poetry Prize*
spring | *Earlier version in* Bluepepper, *May 3rd, 2021*
light and life | Bluepepper *(as 'enlightenmentality'), January 8th, 2016*
Acknowledgement of cover | Kate McNamara
Acknowledgement of photograph, back cover | Conor McNamara

www.ingramcontent.com/pod-product-compliance
Lightning Source LLC
Chambersburg PA
CBHW032023180726
48283CB00008B/2804